MINDSET

John Spera   Tom Johnson

SPECIAL THANKS

Thank you Krissy and Sarah for your continual support. To our children, Riley, Walker, Grace, Breck and Cali, we are proud to call you ours and we work every day to be the example of the people we want you to become. Our investment in the fire service, to include the authoring of this book, only comes through sacrificing valued time with all of you. We cannot begin to imagine where we would be without family.

Thank you to Jay and Jinky Anderson, Craig and Katelyn Stalowy, Sally Johnson, Vicky Mosher, and Lori Clark for their contributions to this book.

CONTENTS

mindset (noun)

/'mīn(d)set/

1. The established set of attitudes held by someone.

2. The foundation of a lifestyle that is in line with whom we want to become.

PREFACE

Oftentimes what separates us from being the firefighter we are and the firefighter we want to be is our mindset. We have built our current mindset based on the things we have allowed to influence us, including past experiences and the work we have done. Over time, this has shaped how we see things. Through this lens, we respond to challenges and circumstances on a daily basis.

Have you ever witnessed a firefighter who sets a goal to lose weight? He writes it down, plans his meals and joins the gym. He is taking all the action steps to be successful but never truly changes his mindset. His old way of thinking, his perception of being fit and what it represents to him, is flawed. This mindset led him to be out of shape in the first place, but he continues to bring it to a new goal, ultimately coming up short because the old thinking produces the same excuses as in the past.

Our mindset is the foundation of a lifestyle that is in line with whom we want to become. It keeps us disciplined to do the necessary daily work to uphold our end of the deal – the oath. This book has been created to help us all develop or reinforce the mindset required to consistently train so that we can serve our communities at the highest level. This performance level is what we would expect from any firefighter who shows up to one of our own homes. Our hope is that this book will assist you in creating and sustaining the discipline to maintain a high standard. Perhaps your mindset is already solid, in which case this book will help you take your training to the next level. It is a book that should be revisited time and time again for those seasons of our careers when the excuses seem to be stronger than our purpose. We believe the pages that follow will position you to overcome the natural human desire to take the path of least resistance and to consistently seek the necessary discomfort to be the firefighter you said you would be.

We Need To Have Our Best
Day On Their Worst Day.

This Doesn't Happen Because
We Want To.

It Happens Because
We Work To.

Chapter 1 – Purpose

John Spera

PASSION LEADS TO PURPOSE

The majority of us have, at one time or another, felt bored in an endeavor or unchallenged by a task. Perhaps we have felt like we are just going through the motions. We look back after a few months or years of being seemingly committed to something, yet we feel unfulfilled and lack passion. Pride in our daily activities is non-existent and we are left to search for something that truly defines us.

We are all able to recognize the firefighter that lacks passion. What exists around the station is not much beyond the art of complaining. There is never investment in the craft and it is always about what is planned off duty rather than what is currently happening on duty. Have you ever asked one of these individuals to define his purpose? Have you asked him what is his *why*? If you did, you would probably receive a muddled response that would ultimately resemble the famous *Billy Madison* movie quote – "What you just said is one of the most insanely idiotic things I have ever heard. At no point in your rambling, incoherent response were you even close to anything that could be considered a rational thought. Everyone in this room is now dumber for having listened to it."

People with passion know their purpose. They can define it readily and clearly. A firefighter that truly is not passionate about something that he spends one-third of his life pursuing is one without purpose, leaving him to wander through life aimlessly. Most of us have the gift of family, and family in part defines us, but it cannot define every part of our existence. We have to seek something greater that builds on family and our chosen profession. We have to connect with a purpose that serves us, fulfills us and guides us through life's ups and downs.

I can honestly say that I traversed through my twenties without purpose. I sought validation from people with whom I had no relationship. I defined myself by external accolades rather than internal satisfactions. For many years I just wanted to be recognized as a top performer in my sport, but due to this, I was always focused on the end result (the recognition) rather than the process. I never sought my purpose, but had I, I would have been content with exercising a relentless work ethic and realizing the benefits that come from it. My teammates would have come first before me. My own self-doubts would have been muted by a confidence for following a passion leading to purpose. Fortunately, I did find my purpose in my thirties. I experienced clarity, and knew exactly what I needed to do. I knew what kind of people I needed to surround myself with, and I accepted the sacrifices I needed to make. As I filtered all actions through my purpose, life's decisions became exponentially simplified.

My purpose centers around my faith, my family, my firefighting career and my desire to seek improvement and knowledge on a daily basis. I define my purpose in three words and I use these words to continually remind myself to stay on course:

Faith – Family – Fire.

Our purpose is our personal mission statement and until it becomes part of the fabric of who we are, we just exist. We have been called to a line of work that has a great responsibility at the heart of it. Being responsible to fight for and protect the lives of others is a great honor, but we must do what is mentally and physically required to fulfill that duty. Purpose gives us a foundation on which to base all our decisions and actions. Purpose provides us something to live for greater than ourselves. It is an anchor in a storm and a lighthouse in the dark. Purpose firmly plants us where we need to be and provides us direction when it is time to move. Having purpose allows us to think and do things with reason. When we have a clear direction, we begin to make decisions that support our purpose and align with our character.

People spend their entire lives pursuing their purpose. Oftentimes, our search is made through jobs, relationships and hobbies that never hit the mark, and we are left feeling unfulfilled. How do we find our purpose? It is a question we ask ourselves daily without even realizing it. It is the one thing that, if we found it, all other things would make sense.

"He who has a why to live for can bear almost any how."

- Friedrich Nietzsche

I cannot define your purpose as a firefighter but I will share mine. I believe that God gave me instincts, both physical and mental, that are best suited to protect others. I realized this at a young age based on the thoughts I had and the activities toward which I gravitated. I found a sense of belonging when I talked about protecting others and I physically trained my body to be able to do just that. I did these things because it is what felt right and what I enjoyed. In other words, I did these things because I was *passionate.*

This was my method of operation regularly while playing games as a kid. We were always battling in the woods and protecting our forts. This type of play consumed my time and, if I did not have to come home for dinner, I would have continued until sunrise the next morning. Sports also provided me with a sense of battling and protecting. We were fighting together as a team against the competition, with a common goal of winning, and I knew that my individual performance would help determine our team's outcome. I felt a sense of responsibility to the team and a feeling of honor when I held up my end of the deal. Simply put, I owned it.

> ☐ *Exercise 1: Take a moment and define your purpose. Put it into words and write it down. Your purpose should define the reason you are here and why you do what you do.*

Why do I bring up my adolescent years? Mostly because many of us share the common background of participating in "war games" as a kid. We all had a mission with the foundation of responsibility. Although many years have passed, it is important to acknowledge how the past reflects many examples of our purpose.

As I grew older, I tried things that were not in line with my purpose. I felt lost and, because of this, nearly everything required forced effort. I did not want to do what I needed to do to live day to day, but I did it anyway because I needed to earn an income, put food on the table and provide shelter, among other things. Comfort, stability and the status quo all had their part in defining where I was prior to finding my purpose.

Fortunately, I found external influences through books and people that started to give me a view of what living with a purpose really looked like. My mind began to shift toward something greater than myself, greater than comfort, stability and the status quo. This led me down a road that caused me to reflect and think, "When am I most happy?"

☐ *Exercise 2: Describe who you are today. Describe the person who you want to be. In order to do this, you have to reflect on your past and how you got to where you are now.*

We believe that we have been called upon to protect the lives of others, and this calling requires us to become the best version of ourselves – mentally, physically and spiritually. Every day I wake up chasing the best version of myself because I know others depend on me. This gives me meaning beyond my own personal feelings. It allows me to do what I need to do even when I do not want to, because it is not about me, but rather it is about all who depend on me to be at my best. Therefore, a fundamental element of my purpose is to be the best version of myself so that I can serve others at the highest level.

Chapter 2 – Belief

Tom Johnson

BELIEF IS BUILT FROM PURPOSE

Ever notice how a historical district in an urban area has beautiful brick homes built over a century ago, and yet, through all these years, they have withstood the test of time? Why has this neighborhood not crumbled? It survives because of two things: its foundation and its continual care and maintenance.

For a firefighter who is just an employee of the organization, three to four decades of service is easy. However, for a firefighter who is a student of the game pursuing greatness, this marathon is nothing short of hard work.

Similar to the historical brick home, to withstand the test of time, a firefighter will need a solid foundation and maintenance, or, as we like to call it – discipline. This foundation of physical, mental and behavioral fitness is predicated on the presence of an unbreakable mindset.

Mind over Matter. We have all heard this phrase, but have we actually witnessed it? What does it look like? Can we buy into this thought process overnight? If you are reading this book hoping for shortcuts to building a strong mindset and mental toughness, then you are reading the wrong book. There are no shortcuts to mental toughness. The truth is mental toughness takes years to develop, but it does not develop without BELIEF.

We BELIEVE that the foundation of any well-rounded firefighter is fitness. We BELIEVE we have complete control over our fitness before we show up for duty or on a fire scene. We BELIEVE that our level of fitness will make the difference between life and death for others. These are not catch phrases for us. We BELIEVE these tenets down to our soul; they are buried within us. Therefore, what we do and how we do it is guided by these beliefs.

> ## "If you don't stand for something you will fall for anything."
>
> ## - Gordon A. Eadie

When conducting recruit academies, it takes discipline to set the alarm for 4 a.m. knowing that at 5 a.m. hard work is on the horizon. As instructors, it can be very easy to shrug off the responsibility of leading by example, and instead sit on the sidelines while our recruits bust their asses during physical training. It is our belief as instructors, specifically our belief in fitness, that ultimately makes it easy for us to get in there with them and model the mindset we want to develop.

Once we have formed that deep-seated belief, it is time to put it into action. We do not just become great firefighters, or, for that matter, great parents or great neighbors, just because we *want* to; we become this because we *work* to. The work we put in every day is an investment. It probably will not pay us back for months or even years, but it will indeed pay us back, with dividends. Our work starts in the gym and on the training ground. It starts with phrases like "this is going to kill us" and "how long are we doing this for?" But if our belief is concrete, then our work ends with "let's do it again, but challenge us more next time."

Our beliefs never allow us to quit. We can fail, but we can NEVER QUIT. In the academy, it never mattered to us if recruits were not the fastest in training – what mattered was that they NEVER QUIT. When we quit, we are training ourselves to quit. Therefore, if we quit in training, we quit on the fire ground. It is as simple as that.

Have you ever quit at something? Have you ever allowed someone close to you, like a child or teammate, to quit something? What follows is a patterned behavior. When things get tough, the quitter says, "I've been here before, and last time I quit." So the quitter quits again. But the opposite also holds true if you train to push on. "I've been here before and I made it through." And this end result breeds success in the future.

Our mental toughness comes from these training experiences and how we perceive them. Do we ever shy away from difficult challenges? Do we embrace failure? If we have failed, did we eventually succeed?

Mental toughness is the ability to say, "We've got this, we've been here before." And we cannot say we've got this if we've never gotten it before. We need to seek out those experiences that will test us and take us to the brink so we can use them in the future and on the fire ground.

"To every man there comes in his lifetime that special moment when he is figuratively tapped on the shoulder and offered the chance to do a very special thing, unique to him and fitted to his talents. What a tragedy if that moment finds him unprepared or unqualified for that which would have been his finest hour."

- **Sir Winston Churchill**

Chapter 3 – Mindset

Tom Johnson

I am not going to sit here and tell you that showing up every day and putting in the hard work is easy. Nothing good in life comes easy. That last statement calls for more attention, so think about it. If I handed you a badge and told you, "Congratulations, you are now a firefighter, you are the luckiest person on the planet to have fallen into a job like this," what would you say?

I just told myself that exact statement and instinctively rolled my eyes. I sure as hell did not earn that badge, so I do not want it. But what if we pushed you to your max for four to six months while you sacrificed your time with loved ones, and you gave up many things you hold dear to make it happen? In this case, you earned the badge. It is a much different story on graduation day. You could not be prouder. Remember, NOTHING GOOD IN LIFE COMES EASY.

It will not be easy to show up every day nor should it be. If I counted how many times in the last year I have started off a day with complete excitement toward training and physical activity, it would be on one hand. So why do I get in there every day? The answer is discipline. This belief we have in physical, mental and behavioral fitness has led to the discipline necessary to see it through for many years. And let's be clear − motivation is not what we are talking about. Motivation and discipline are two entirely different concepts.

Motivation is short-term, while discipline is long-term.

We all know that firefighter who excelled in the academy and two years later has a lazy reputation. He possessed the motivation in the academy, but lacked the discipline. When we talk about those people with mental toughness, we are not talking about motivated individuals; we are talking about disciplined individuals.

"I am the master of my fate: I am the captain of my soul."

- **William Ernest Henley**

Motivation is guaranteed to sell you short over a 30-year career in the fire service, but discipline will be there at the finish line. So those other 360 days of the year I am not motivated to train, I rely on discipline to show up. It gets the job done every time.

Results matter. To be honest, results in the weight room, on the running track or on the sports field do not matter. Yes, they are a component to the overall development of firefighter fitness, but the great equalizer is the fire ground. We cannot cheat on the fire ground. The job either gets done successfully or it does not. So when we measure results, measure them on the fire ground. Everything we do on a daily basis should be geared toward yielding positive results on the fire ground. We can bench 350 pounds, but can we move charged 2-1/2" hose for more than five minutes or perform vertical ventilation under time constraints? We can run a five minute mile, but can we lift a lifeless victim to the window sill from the floor?

BELIEF = MINDSET

MINDSET = DISCIPLINE

DISCIPLINE = RESULTS

Our mindset toward training and life in general is the key to success. Our view of training cannot be one where we dread the very thought of it. We have to embrace it. We have to understand that it is going to get uncomfortable, but we must get comfortable being uncomfortable because this is where personal growth lies.

Years ago, a college coach of mine addressed the team during fall workouts and said something that resonated with me. At the time, I did not understand the significance of it, but with every year that passes, it rings truer. Tony Cirelli said, "Get comfortable being uncomfortable." In that context, he simply meant if you want to get better, you are going to have to change. You are going to have to change a lot while you play for this team, so you must believe in that thought process.

At that time, firefighting was not on my list of to-do's in life. What my coach said then to the team is arguably more beneficial to a firefighter than a baseball player. As a baseball player, it just meant changing mechanics, learning new pitches or approaching an at-bat differently. As a firefighter, it means swallowing your pride, shelving your ego and exposing your weaknesses. If you truly want to become a better firefighter, you have to get comfortable being uncomfortable.

Get Comfortable Being Uncomfortable.

What does this really mean on a day-to-day basis? It starts in workouts. It means participating in a workout that is not suited to our talents. For example, it could be running, burpees or rowing. If we are weaker at these exercises, chances are we resist them, and we avoid the discomfort that comes with them. This same decision carries over to the training ground, except now it is climbing stairs, throwing ladders or moving 2-1/2" hose. We shy away from these tasks because they are outside our comfort zone.

This decision creates a vicious cycle within firefighters. We do not like to perform a skill because we are not as good at it as we would like to be, so we seldom do it. Because we seldom do it, the skill gets rusty, creating more apprehension in practicing or performing the skill. Now, we are essentially afraid of it. This can happen even on the smallest scale, such as donning our bunker gear and SCBA. This lack of training is sometimes mislabeled as complacency or laziness, but more often than not it is simply a fear of failure, a fear of looking bad in front of our peers or a fear of exposing a weakness we deny is there.

If our goal is truly to be outstanding students of the game, we have to put ourselves in learning and growth situations. Remember one final thought from my former Italian coach: "Niente buon è facile." Nothing good is easy.

The Standard.

Never Lower Your Standard.
Inspire Others To
Raise Theirs.

Chapter 4 – Responsibility

John Spera & Tom Johnson

One of our favorite quotes comes from Thomas Edison. "Opportunity is missed by most people because it is dressed in overalls and looks like work." In the fire service, most people have not missed that opportunity when it comes to initially landing this career. We did the work in order to get the opportunity to wear this uniform.

During the hiring process and our initial recruit academy, we are creating opportunity left and right. We are showing up every day, owning the career and investing in the organization. We do not believe we are entitled to anything. We learn a ton, and we are establishing a reputation that will stay with us for an entire career, which at times may or may not be a blessing.

> ## "Opportunity is missed by most people because it is dressed in overalls and looks like work."
>
> ## - Thomas Edison

That being said, opportunity seems to miss a healthy percentage of firefighters once on the job. Why is that? Is it departmental politics? Is it personality conflicts? Is it bad luck? Quite honestly, it is none of these. It ties right back to

Edison – it is missed by most because it is dressed in bunkers, and it is work. Hard work.

OWNERSHIP

"This new generation of firefighters is entitled." At least that is what the old generation of firefighters is saying. We have worked with the old generation and we have trained the new generation, and we feel that before we talk about entitlement we should first address ownership. Regardless of the roles we have within our own departments, we must ask ourselves if we truly own these roles? Do we believe everything that happens on our watch is our responsibility? If we train a recruit or a probationary firefighter, do we believe their success is a representation of our instruction or mentoring? Do we own the actions of our crew like we own the actions of our own family?

All too commonly heard around the firehouse is, "We never train because my officer does not like to." However, sometimes it is the senior guy or the engineer that runs the show, not the officer. Is this our reason for not keeping our skills up, because the officer or senior firefighter runs the days without prioritizing training? Our skills, knowledge and abilities have to be maintained consistently, and blaming this lack of discipline on someone else is an excuse. Owning our career means never blaming someone else for our shortcomings.

The way we see it, those who complain about the new generation or the entitlement in the fire service simply do not own the position they hold. If things go south on a fire scene, we often hear everyone quick to blame the officer because he did not give the firefighters operational expectations. Did those firefighters seek out those expectations from their officer? Were they as aggressive in obtaining expectations as they were in operating on the fire ground? It is as much the responsibility of officers to lay out expectations for their crews as it is for the firefighters to seek out these expectations. And it goes both ways – the officer should be asking what the crew's expectations are as well.

If you are an officer, but you cannot seem to get things done *because of the Chief,* then you are a manager and not a leader. You have the title, but that is as far as it takes you. A leader finds a way to get it done. If negativity devours your crew daily, it is not administration's fault; rather, it is your fault as the leader. Taking ownership of what happens in your station and on your truck is a necessity if you wish to create change and opportunity for yourself and those with whom you work. Prioritizing the team goals over your own is the foundation of a great fire company and a great culture. Without a doubt, there are no bad crews, just bad officers.

Lead Yourself Before You Lead Others.

INVESTMENT

If we deposit money into a savings account, it takes time to receive a return on our investment. We sacrifice the use of that money for the foreseeable future to realize gains and benefits years down the road. We know not to expect the same returns realized by others who invested their savings twenty years prior. They have put the time in while we are just beginning. We also know that if we only put money into savings right now, and we do not continue to invest more money on a regular basis, our return will be quite minimal.

We struggle in the fire service with investing in our department and the future. For example, we can have two years of experience but expect the returns from our department that are received by a 20-year firefighter. At the same time, for the 20-year firefighter, it can sometimes be assumed that initial deposits will return significant gains without any further investment. How can we have it so backward? The profession of firefighting is no different than any other when it comes to return on investment. The more we put in, the more we get paid back – maybe not instantaneously and maybe not monetarily, but we will get paid back. It is guaranteed.

Think about raising children. It takes a ton of sacrifice, time and effort on the front end, especially for the first five to seven years. At some point, the investment we put into our children begins to pay us back. We start to see growth and maturity, and they start to send some appreciation our way (at least until those dreaded teenage years!). The point is that this investment in our children does not pay dividends overnight. It never has and never will. The savings account never pays dividends overnight – never has, never will. And guess what – the fire service is exactly the same.

FIND A POSITION OF INFLUENCE

We regularly hear suggestions from firefighters of all ranks on new ideas, tactics and policies that should be implemented. More often than not, there is a position within the department that is responsible for the implementation of such suggestion(s), and therefore there is opportunity. But when offered that opportunity, the response is usually negative.

A few years back, we sat down with a well-respected officer in our organization and he told us, "At some point, you have to give back to the organization that has given to you." It really has to be a selfless goal, one that puts the organization ahead of the individual. To parallel sports, it is about emphasizing the name on the front of the jersey and not the back. John F. Kennedy demonstrated this concept over half a century ago when he famously stated to our great country, "Ask not what your country can do for you, ask what you can do for your country." So stop asking what the department or the city you work for is doing for you. Start asking what you can do for them.

It only takes a few years in the fire service to understand that the old saying, "One hundred years of tradition unimpeded by progress," is more truth than not. Changing anything in the fire service takes time and patience, but the good news is we can create this change from any position. We do not need to be the Chief or the officer; we just need to create opportunity through influence, and influence is garnered over time. Others see how we lead ourselves, and they see how our core values and beliefs are not compromised regardless of the company we keep. Inherently, people gravitate toward those who are confident in their decisions and actions, and are also humble enough to know they cannot do it alone. We may only be able to influence one person in our organization over the next year. However, over time that number will grow exponentially if the goal of our thoughts and actions is to better the organization.

Finally, it comes down to simple perspective. If we do not like work, we will see organizational challenges as barriers to success. On the other hand, if we do like work, we will be blessed with countless opportunities in the fire service, and in life in general. Create your own opportunities, make an impact and change your organization for the better through hard work and giving back.

RESPONDING TO NO

Perspective is everything. *No* does not literally mean no. It means Next Opportunity. Since change is so tough to come by in the fire service, we say you have not hit the starting line until you have been told *no* a dozen times. Hearing *no*, especially when it is something we are passionate about, is never easy. We are tied emotionally to our thoughts and proposals, but the key is formulating a plan, and then moving to Plan B, C or even Plan D when roadblocks present themselves. "Plan A Harder" or quitting are not options.

Implementing a fitness assessment at our department was a five year process. Calling that a commitment would be an understatement. It took patience and an unwavering vision for the future. Through this period of change, we ran into countless individuals who would try to sabotage our efforts, minimize the importance of it or just flat out waste our time. We realized that these people were loud, but they were the bottom 20% in our profession that never have and never will show any interest in the fire service and its progression. We did not waste our time on them. We kept moving forward and focused on the other 80%, knowing we would not have to worry about buy-in from the top 20%. Not only did the top 20% know why our cause was important, they too understood our commitment level because they were involved in their own endeavors that mirrored ours.

It is the middle 60% that will change the culture of any department, and therefore we directed our efforts toward this group. Delivery and approach were key to creating buy-in when we were selling fitness to our department. We truly believed it was about getting better, and starting points for some were different than for others. Everyone knew that no matter where they began, they had support.

There Is No Need To Tell
People What You Are
All About.

Your Actions Tell Them
Everything They Need
To Know.

Chapter 5 – Performance

John Spera & Tom Johnson

DEFINITION OF SUCCESS

How do we define success? Defining it based on rank or salary will leave us feeling empty time and time again. What if we measured success by our level of influence and the impact we have on the careers of others? What if we factored in our crew's performance on the fire ground or at major emergency scenes? Or even more telling, what if the crew's success was measured only when we were not there? Sure, everything goes smoothly when we are in charge, but what happens when we are on vacation? Does the crew keep operating without missing a beat?

To a great extent, our own success should be defined and measured through others. The progression of our co-workers throughout their careers should be a major benchmark as a leader in the fire service. The aim should not be to occupy the front seat and *control* everyone's decisions and actions; rather it should be to *facilitate* their individual needs and goals. The good leaders create more leaders to work alongside them. Much better results are yielded when everyone within the crew is given the freedom to present ideas, direct trainings and have input in decision making, while at the same time knowing that the officer supports growth through an acceptable level of risk and mistakes. When looking for answers, we never point to our bugles. Instead, we develop our people so we can point to them for the answers.

YES VS. NO

Saying *no* to members of our own organization is the easiest thing to do as a chief, company officer or leader, and not surprisingly, nothing good comes from it. We have essentially eliminated any issues, complaints, requests for needs or resources, or any responsibility whatsoever to our people. Remember in Chapter 3 when we talked about nothing good in life comes easy? Well, saying *no* is easy.

Yes, on the other hand, is hard. *Yes* requires us to stay committed to a request and facilitate the needs of that firefighter, crew or cadre. For example, a firefighter approaches the organization with an idea of how to recruit a diverse pool of applicants at the high school level. She has a plan to foster relationships with the school leaders and also to interact with the students at various functions. *She has taken ownership.* Saying *no* eliminates the leader's responsibility and commitment to this firefighter, and although it makes the leader's life easier, it frustrates the firefighter to no end. Talent and ambition are stifled, and this can sometimes lead the firefighter to feel disenfranchised. With *yes*, we empower our people and allow them to take ownership. Of course it is more work for everyone, but that hard work is what brings out the good things in the fire service.

When leading, we challenge you to say *yes*. As much as you can, say *yes*. *Yes* opens doors for the team and creates learning opportunities for everyone.

THE POWER OF FAILURE

There is a difference between failing due to a lack of preparation and failing due to pushing the envelope. The former can be tied to complacency or inability, while the latter can only yield growth and strong mindset development.

"Sometimes you must sacrifice yourself on the altar of effort to be reminded of what and who you could become if you applied yourself."

\- **Mark Twight**

We know from our youth and from making mistakes that we typically learn more from our mistakes than we do from our successes. So why do we fear making mistakes when we train for our profession? Obviously ego plays a big part, but more than that is our perspective on life. Those of us who hide from drills and activities that may expose our weaknesses have a short-sighted mindset. We only see the negativity that immediately follows a mistake, whether it be from peers or from internal thoughts and feelings. What we miss is the long-term benefit of improving over time. We sacrifice our chance to improve for the feeling of comfort. Too often comfort prevents a firefighter from trying a new skill, an officer from speaking the truth or a Chief from leading his people before serving the boss above.

Remember the majority of the greatest all-time success stories in history were preceded by failure. Abraham Lincoln failed in business in 1831, suffered a nervous breakdown in 1836, and was later defeated in his run for Vice President in 1856. We all know what happened next time he ran for President. One of Walt Disney's earlier ventures, Laugh-o-Gram Studios, went bankrupt due to his inability to run a successful business. Disney was also fired from a Missouri newspaper for lack of creativity, but his dreams eventually came to fruition. Michael Jordan was cut from his high school varsity basketball team as a sophomore, but it is safe to say he "rebounded" from that setback quite well.

Once we start to embrace failure as a tool to get better, the growth in our personal and professional lives will be unmatched. We start looking at pressure situations as challenges instead of threats. We stop caring about those on the sideline who do not train, let alone those who do not even dress out in bunker gear. We stop caring about those who say we cannot do something on the fire ground just because they refuse to or are unable to do it themselves. We become change agents, even if it is on the smallest scale.

CHECKING THE EGO

When we train to win, we are bound to fail at some point. How we handle failure is the determining factor in improving. Too often, when we train in front of our peers, we take the easy road or the less challenging one. This presents predictable results that enable us to "high-five" at the end, and our egos do not take a hit. Not only have we not improved, but the gap between who we think we are and who we actually are has widened even more.

The goal of any training should be to expose weaknesses and then target them so they are no longer shortcomings. So when we are nervous about throwing ladders or participating in high rise training, realize that is exactly what we should be doing. If we are apprehensive at performing a skill, we are weak at the skill. If it excites us to pull the ladder off the truck, or it excites us to hike 15 flights of stairs in order to move charged 2-1/2" hose, then we know we have prepared. It is about training outside of the comfort zone. We have to design our training to be a surprise so that it challenges us.

So many times we see miserable firefighters around the station not enjoying the job like they did in years prior. Why was the job so fun then, but now seems to be a burden? If you were a real estate agent, and you only sold two houses per year, we would all agree that you are not very good at your job. We would bet that you probably do not like to come to work. Every potential client you meet with confirms you are not good at your job when they choose another agent instead of you. So you have two choices: you can quit or you can look in the mirror and get better. Getting better in the realtor's case means seeking out continuing education classes, finding a mentor to shadow and getting more aggressive with sales leads. Getting better for a firefighter means getting outside and training! It means looking in the mirror and realizing you are not the firefighter your ego says you are.

It is really simple. Most firefighters who used to love the job, but no longer do, have apprehension related to their skills and performance. It is not fun to do things we are not good at. Since there has been very little practice over the years, these firefighters hide from training because it exposes them and their weaknesses. Egos have simply gotten in the way.

We have heard many times over the years that, as probationary firefighters, we will be our smartest and best right out of the academy because we have been practicing every day for months. Do not fall for this! Every day we should be getting better, and the firefighters we are today should be far better than the ones who graduated from the academy. If we train to win, we undoubtedly will be much better firefighters.

The Day Will Come When You Have To Prove That You Are The Firefighter You Believe Yourself To Be.

Will You Be Ready?

Chapter 6 – Train To Win

John Spera & Tom Johnson

In our current society, winning is frowned upon at times. Occasionally we can be made to feel shallow for pursuing the top prize. And if we do not earn the top prize, we are usually rewarded with some version of a participation trophy. But when it comes to the fire ground, life and death are on the line. Winning is paramount. There are no participation trophies.

The one thing that never changes on each fire is the opponent. It is us versus fire. The one thing we can control before we show up to any fire is our level of fitness and training. So in this case, it is up to us to do the work to prepare.

PRACTICE THE AUDIBLE

Our profession parallels sports in many ways. We must refine our skills regularly to be ready for the big game. Our Super Bowl or Game 7 may only come once or twice a year, similar to professional athletes. However we do not have spring training, preseason, regular season, or even playoffs. We practice plays (evolutions like forward hose lays and vertical ventilation), but more often than not, there is no defense (such as the fire) and we do not have a play clock. Seldom do we have rehearsed audibles when things go bad. Our *Plan A* turns into *Plan A Harder* and we have not developed the ability to move on to *Plan B, C or D*. If we do not audible in training, how can we expect to audible on the fire ground?

Case in point, in 2016, a second alarm fire at a multi-family building produced a fatality and a firefighter mayday. A failure of the FDC led to Plan B, which meant creating a "standpipe" using the aerial ladder pipe, and stretching off of that to the floor below, then to the fire floor. The mayday and the FDC failure occurred simultaneously. Quick decisions were made by those operating on the fire ground, and the snowball that was a problem on scene was prevented from becoming an avalanche. Every fire is different, and none go as planned. There are always mistakes or delays or miscommunications, but the best firefighters and the best crews are the ones who deal with these issues and correct them in the shortest amount of time, not letting them derail the entire incident.

PROFESSIONAL OR AMATUER

Many fire departments have mission statements that in one way or another contain something about "professionals." We consider ourselves professionals, and we are tactical athletes, but are we putting in the training similar to other professional athletes? Remember, professionals have skills and abilities that the general public does not, and professionals spend hours a day honing their craft. Can we say that we are professional firefighters?

TRAIN FOR THE GAME

We are placed in very physically demanding environments that require an extraordinary amount of work, and only professional firefighters have the ability to perform at a high level. The physical demands placed on our bodies are one of the most extreme imaginable due to the internal and external environments within which we operate. Internally, we perform as tactical athletes covered by 60 to 70 pounds of gear that traps heat and raises our body temperature to over 101 degrees Fahrenheit. Due to this core temperature rise, we start to lose pattern recognition and recall. We experience peripheral narrowing and auditory exclusion. Why would we not want to experience these physiological changes as much as possible prior to showing up for our Super Bowl?

It Is Irresponsible And Unacceptable To Show Up Out Of Shape. It's Not Personal, It's Professional.

Our external environment is one that can take a human life in seconds and is constantly changing. A room and contents fire can develop to flashover in 60 to 90 seconds, so <u>time</u> is our enemy. Are we timing ourselves and our crew when we perform tasks on the training ground? Do we know how long it takes to VES a second floor bedroom? Do we know how long it will take us to reach the seat of the fire from the time we arrive on scene? We have seen some crews complete basic tasks in two minutes, while others take three times longer for the same tasks. Worse yet, sometimes the tasks do not even get completed. If fire doubles in size every 30 seconds (and that is probably conservative), then what kind of opponent will the two minute crew face on the inside of a structure compared to the six minute crew? It is the difference between life and death – for everyone!

Imagine your favorite NFL football team preparing for the Super Bowl. If they were never in pads, never practiced against a live defense and never practiced in front of a crowd, would you bet on them to win? What if this team spent most of its days just talking about the playbook and drawing "Xs and Os" instead of actually running the plays? What if they only practiced once a month? There is a reason professional teams practice with crowd noise and against a live defense. They are preparing for the environment in which they will be playing. Common sense, right? Fire training should be no different.

Competency Yields The Highest Level Of Safety On The Fire Ground, Not Aversion.

UNPREPARED IS UNSAFE

Safety has become paramount on fire scenes over the past few decades. But is it really safe to show up to a fire unprepared? If we want to increase safety on the fire ground for firefighters and decrease the risk of injury or death, then practice how we play! When we practice how we play, we only get better because we are guaranteed to confront some degree of failure. And these failures are opportunities to learn and get better. Failing on the training ground is much more preferable than failing on the fire ground.

RUNNING ON THE FIRE GROUND

Crawl – Walk – Run. This is the formula for learning. This methodology is dead on for the fire service. We should be refining the basic skills after we learn them, and then always be working to perform them faster and more efficiently. As retired FDNY firefighter Kevin Shea says, "Master the basics until they become advanced."

"Master the basics until they become advanced."

- **Kevin Shea**

There are plenty of options when it comes to techniques for forcible entry, search, deploying hose lines or any fire ground skills. Stop trying to practice the next best thing. Pick two or three ways to do something and achieve mastery of those. It takes daily practice of these skills to stay at peak performance.

Current and former athletes understand what it means to train to win. They have been part of a team where preparation for competition is the priority. They understand that if they are not working to get better, they are regressing. At the same time, their competition is getting better while they sit idly by. The same can be said for an engine company's battle with the fire. Fire is constantly evolving, whether it is the spaces it is burning inside the structure or the materials it ignites. It is always "getting better." Are we able to step onto the same playing field as our opponent in this case and compete? If we are not consistently training to win, the answer is no.

If fire is evolving, so must we. We were taught in the academy to never run on the fire ground, but that was the academy and we were rookies. That was D League, or the minors; now we have to compete in the big leagues. It is time to take our game to the next level. Running on the fire ground enables us to make up seconds and even minutes on the outside, so that conditions are potentially better on the inside – for THEM. And guess what – it is better for us too.

"Appearance is the consequence of fitness, and confidence is the consequence of capability."

- **Mark Twight**

EMBRACE COMPETITION

If you have never competed in any sport or been part of any team that practices physical work or skills, the thought of competition can be unsettling. You may have never won or lost in your life, and competition and the stress that comes with it can turn you off. But if we – yes, we – are going to get better, it is going to take effort from everyone on the crew. Understanding that competition makes us all better is the most important fact. For centuries, in any industry, competition has been the driving force for improvement across the globe. We competed to be the first country to put a man on the moon. We compete to put the best electronics product out on the market. We compete to run the fastest mile. In training, we suffer highs and lows because of this, but that is all part of the process. All along the way, we are building mental toughness and giving ourselves a better shot at victory on the fire ground.

Is it about winning and losing? YES! If we are not winning on the fire ground, we are losing. In training environments, winning is fine but losing is where we learn. In the end, however, it is not firefighters that win or lose the competition; it is the citizens of the community. If we are competing to get better, the citizens we serve ultimately win – every time!

Train To Win.

Fire Doesn't Hand Out
Participation Trophies.

AFTERWORD

The Standard. What is your standard? What kind of firefighter do you want to be?

We work every day trying to become the firefighter we would want showing up at our own home. Honestly, we do not know if we will ever be as good as we want to be at throwing ladders, stretching hose or forcing doors. It is the relentless training of a firefighter, drenched in sweat to the point of complete exhaustion when no one else is watching, that truly honors the oath.

Our thought progression, through consistently seeking discomfort and challenging ourselves, will evolve to the point that we will begin to feel uncomfortable while in situations of comfort. Just going through the motions will now be uncomfortable. This is the next level of growth.

Knowing we will never be satisfied or feel as though we have reached the pinnacle, we will be chasing a better version of ourselves every day. It is this pursuit that best defines our standard.

Would You Want You Rescuing You?

NOTES

NOTES

NOTES

Printed in Poland
by Amazon Fulfillment
Poland Sp. z o.o., Wrocław